Out of this WORLD

SATURN
Amazing Rings

by Chaya Glaser

Consultant: Karly M. Pitman, PhD
Planetary Science Institute
Tucson, Arizona

BEARPORT PUBLISHING

New York, New York

Credits
Cover, © NASA/JPL/Space Science Institute; TOC, © NASA/JPL/Space Science Institute;
4–5, © NASA/JPL/Space Science Institute; 6–7, © Wikipedia & NASA; 8, © NASA/JPL/
Space Science Institute; 9, © Juergen Faelchle/Shutterstock; 10–11, © NASA/JPL/
Space Science Institute; 12, © NASA and The Hubble Heritage Team (STScI/AURA)
Acknowledgment: R.G. French (Wellesley College), J. Cuzzi (NASA/Ames), L. Dones (SwRI),
and J. Lissauer (NASA/Ames); 13, © image courtesy of CALTECH/NASA; 14, © NASA/
JPL; 15, © NASA/JPL/Space Science Institute; 16–17, © NASA/JPL–Caltech/SSI/Cornell;
18–19, © NASA/JPL/Space Science Institute; 19, © NASA/JPL/University of Colorado;
20–21, © Courtesy of NASA and Space Science Institute; 23TL, © iStock/Thinkstock; 23TR,
© Wikipedia & NASA; 23BL, © NASA/JPL; 23BR, © NASA/JPL.

Publisher: Kenn Goin
Editor: Jessica Rudolph
Creative Director: Spencer Brinker
Design: Deborah Kaiser
Photo Researcher: Michael Win

Library of Congress Cataloging-in-Publication Data

Glaser, Chaya, author.
  Saturn : amazing rings / by Chaya Glaser.
      pages cm. — (Out of this world)
  Includes bibliographical references and index.
  ISBN 978-1-62724-566-1 (library binding) — ISBN 1-62724-566-9 (library binding)
  1. Planetary rings—Juvenile literature. 2. Saturn (Planet)—Juvenile literature. I. Title.
  QB671.G53 2015
  523.46—dc23
                                    2014034614

For more information, write to Bearport Publishing Company, Inc., 45 West 21st Street, Suite 3B,
New York, New York 10010. Printed in the United States of America.

10 9 8 7 6 5 4 3 2 1

CONTENTS

Which planet has
many bright rings?

SATURN!

5

Saturn is part of Earth's Solar System.

JUPiTER

MARS

VENUS

EARTH

MERCURY

SUN

SATURN

URANUS

NEPTUNE

It's the sixth planet
from the Sun.

Saturn is huge.

SATURN

EARTH

It is so big that 763 Earths could fit inside it!

A thick layer of gases surrounds Saturn.

The gases give the planet its colors.

Some parts are yellow.

Other parts are blue.

Saturn is much windier than Earth.

Winds on Earth can reach 318 miles per hour (512 kph).

Winds on Saturn can blow at up to 1,100 miles per hour (1,770 kph)!

A giant, windy storm on Saturn

People have not visited Saturn.

However, spacecraft have explored the planet.

A spacecraft

They sent information
back to Earth.

Saturn has at least
12 rings.

The rings orbit,
or move around,
the planet.

Rings

Saturn's rings are made of pieces of ice and rock.

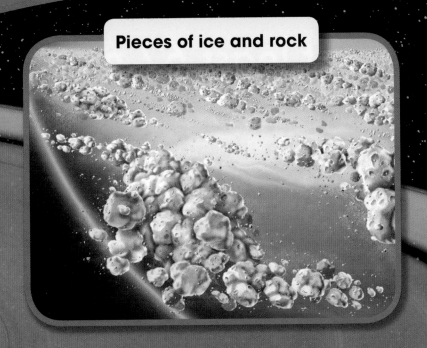

Pieces of ice and rock

Some pieces are smaller than a grain of sand.

Some are bigger than a house.

At least 62 moons
orbit Saturn.

Scientists think there are more moons and rings to discover!

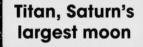
Titan, Saturn's largest moon

SATURN

VERSUS

EARTH

SATURN		EARTH
Sixth planet from the Sun	**POSITION**	Third planet from the Sun
72,367 miles (116,463 km) across	**SIZE**	7,918 miles (12,743 km) across
About −288°F (−178°C)	**AVERAGE TEMPERATURE**	59°F (15°C)
62	**NUMBER OF MOONS**	One

GLOSSARY

gases (GASS-iz)   substances that float in the air and are neither liquid nor solid; many gases are invisible

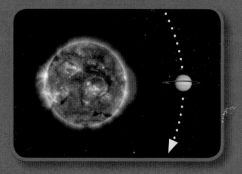

orbit (OR-bit)   to circle around a planet, the Sun, or another object

Solar System (SOH-lur SISS-tuhm)   the Sun and everything that circles around it, including the eight planets

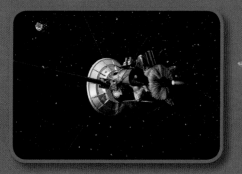

spacecraft (SPAYSS-kraft)   vehicles that can travel in space

INDEX

READ MORE

Lawrence, Ellen. *Saturn: The Ringed Wonder (Zoom Into Space).* New York: Ruby Tuesday Books (2014).

Taylor-Butler, Christine. *Saturn (Scholastic News Nonfiction Readers).* New York: Children's Press (2005).

LEARN MORE ONLINE

To learn more about Saturn, visit
www.bearportpublishing.com/OutOfThisWorld

ABOUT THE AUTHOR

Chaya Glaser enjoys looking up at the stars and reading stories about the constellations. When she's not admiring the night sky, she can be found playing musical instruments.